I'm Kind of a Big Deal

~

Mitch Wakem

PublishAmerica
Baltimore

At the specific preference of the author, PublishAmerica allowed this work to remain exactly as the author intended, verbatim, without editorial input.

ISBN: 1-4241-8133-X
PUBLISHED BY PUBLISHAMERICA, LLLP
www.publishamerica.com
Baltimore

Printed in the United States of America

I'm Kind of a Big Deal

~

MitchWakem

Table of Contents

So It Begins 7

Animal Crackers 10

I'm Kind of a Big Deal 15

The Ervin Factor 19

Do You Come Here Often? 25

First Dates Are Interviews 33

Wanna Make Out? 38

Trust Me 44

Come and Talk to Me 50

Breaking Down the Wall 55

The Little Things 60

It's Not You, It's Me 63

And I'm Spent 74

SO IT BEGINS

So I'm at the bookstore looking for the latest James Patterson novel and happen to walk through the *Love and Relationships* section of the store. I always like to take a second or two to browse the titles, not because I'm looking for advice, more so that I always like to hear what the people who are too busy writing books have to say about relationships. The book they have on display is none other than *Dr. Phil McGraw's, "Love Smart: Find the one you want-fix the one you got."* I have to be honest this made me chuckle a little, for a few simple reasons. The first being, have you ever actually thought about Dr. Phil as some sort of smooth relationship guy? *Hell No!* And more so the fact that Dr. Phil always seems to have the answers, or so he leads people to believe. Have you ever watched his show, the guy is an asshole, how does that help people?

I'm not going to lash in to a personal attack on Dr. Phil, but let's be honest here. He is simply using what he's learned from some text book that was written by some guy who hasn't been laid since Columbus and the Mayflower set sail. He is simply another doctor who thinks because he spent a life time in school and the rest of his time reading the Psychological Science Journal, that it has earned him to right to tell us the best way to live our lives.

The second book that caught my attention is one that I have actually read myself, *Daniel Goleman's Social Intelligence: The New Science of Human Relationships.* This book is rather unique in its theory's of relationships and human interaction. I'll save you the $20 that the book costs and explain Goleman's theory in a sentence. Daniel believes that we connect brain to brain, sending emotions and signals from one person to another. While I won't even pretend to understand the full capabilities of the human brain, I find flaws to this theory. If the brain is sending out emotions, then why is it that when a guy hits on a girl at a bar, and she's not interested, why does the guy continue to pursue her. Under Goleman's theory wouldn't the girl's brain just send out the "Go to hell, creep" vibe? And for that matter why doesn't the guy's brain get this vibe and move on to find a girl who's so drunk that his pickup lines may be construed as flattering? Sorry Goleman there is just too many unanswered questions to your theory.

There were in excess of forty books on the shelf in that section of the store, all of them written by some doctor or someone who claims to be an expert on the subject. I browsed most of these books, forgetting about getting the new Patterson novel. I found much more entertainment with these books then I could ever get from Mr. Patterson (who happens to be my favorite author so that certainly is no knock on James). Most of these books that claim to be self help books, all seem to offer some sure fire way to turn your love life around, whether you're happily married or out looking for love. Like there is a secret answer that they hand to you in a fortune cookie the day you get your PHD. Get real; there is no well-defined answer to everyone's relationship problems because everyone's problems are unique.

So I decided it was time for a book about relationships to be written by a normal person. Someone who's had his heart stepped on, and has done the two-step on a few hearts of his own. For most of us, when we have relationship problems, and need advice, do we run to some doctor who knows nothing about us personally? No, we go to our friends, or more specifically, we go to that one friend who always seems to have the right answers. (Strangely enough the friend is usually single.) This book is going to be written from that state of mind—I will be that friend you go to for answers, and contently enough, I just so happen to be single.

I'm not a doctor and with the exception of Halloween I don't even pretend to be one. Although I wouldn't mind playing a doctor on one of those daytime soap operas—the doctor always gets all kinds of action. I have no intentions of throwing six syllable words at you. This is going to be simple and easy to understand. After all, love is complicated enough as it is, why make it harder by having to look up every other word in this book. There will probably be more typographical errors in this book than you would ever expect. I'm going to take you in to the basic principles of dating, as I see them. At the same time, I'm going to use real life stories, my stories; so don't laugh because I've been through some crazy relationships. Well, I want you to laugh, just not at me, laugh with me.

So get yourself a beverage (an Adult one if you're of age or from Canada) kick back in your favorite chair with a box of tissue and open your mind up a little, surely my thoughts and opinions are not going to appeal to everyone and that's expected, but I think there is something everyone can take from this book, even if it's just the smallest of things, I truly believe there is some relevant information you can gather from this book. And if for some reason you can take nothing useful from this book, the worst case scenario is you laugh a lot, so what is there to lose?

ANIMAL CRACKERS

"We always believe our first love is our last,
and our last love our first."
—Mitch Wakem (yeah I said that)

I was sitting at my computer late one night eating Animal Crackers (which I strongly feel should be a cookie. They are sweet after all and you can get them with frosting on them—have you ever heard of any other frosted crackers? Think about it, frosted saltines—Yummy! But I digress) Anyway I was sitting at my computer, eating animal crackers and thinking. I came to realize the answer to one of the world's most pondered questions—the meaning of life. Now allow me to explain completely before you judge or dismiss my theory.

Truthfully it's rather simple, as a matter of fact, I can answer this pensive question with a one-word answer. Yeah, that's right one word to sum up yours, mine, and everyone else's existence in this world. Now before I reveal that one word I would like you to take a moment and open your mind up a bit. Sit down, take a few deep breaths, count to ten and break out that bottle of Scotch you've been saving for a special occasion. Prepare yourself to take things in, I'm not going to blow your mind, you know this word. I'm sure you use it daily, most people do. This one word has such a vast meaning, you could ask twenty people to define it and

I'm almost willing to bet that you won't get the same answer more than twice. As a matter of fact, the dictionary has about seventeen different definitions for the word, one of them being (and I quote), "Attraction based on sexual desire."

The word if you haven't guessed it by now is **LOVE**. Gandhi once said, or maybe twice who knows for sure; *"Where there is love there is life."* So it would make sense that where there is life there is love—yes!?

Think about it for a second, there are very few things in this world that we all have in common (other than breathing and dying). So why couldn't love be that single purpose that we all have in this world? Some might say that it's too simple—but is it really? Anyone who's ever been in love could tell you that it is often complicated and confusing. They would tell you there is nothing simple about the word love. It's such a complicated emotion that we can't even clearly define it. Think about the lengths that people go to for love, and I'm not talking about the corny stuff they do in Tom Hanks and Meg Ryan movies. You know psychologists say that well over 50% of suicides are rooted from love or lack thereof. They don't have families to love them, or they lost that special boyfriend or girlfriend. To those people that love was so meaningful, that without it, life had no meaning in itself.

Abu Hamid Muhammad Al-Ghazzali (who was one of the greatest philosophers of his time. 1058-1111) said this about love:

"Are you ready to cut off your head and place your foot on it? If so, come; Love awaits you! Love is not grown in a garden, nor sold in the marketplace; whether you are a king or a servant, the price is your head, and nothing less. Yes, the cost of the elixir of

love is your head! Do you hesitate? Oh miser, it is cheap at that price!"

What would you do for love? The better question would be, what wouldn't you do for love?

But it's not as simple as it sounds really. Think about Love, how many times have you said it in your life? To how many people? Well let's discount anything from before the time you were fifteen, and we'll eliminate family members and your invisible friend (who, for the record was probably a dirty pirate hooker, lord knows mine was!) Lets just look at the number of people we've said it to in a romantic state. So what is the number? Don't say one cause I'll have to call you a liar. Hell, love is the most over used word in the English language—"Oh I love these shoes!!" or "I love pizza!" We, as humans, seem to fall in love with physical objects so don't try to tell me that you've only told one person that you loved them in a romantic sense. (Unless you're one of those few people who have been dating the same person since you were fifteen. If that's the case, maybe you've only said it once. And I'd love to talk to you more about that, as well.) Be honest with yourself, no one is going to call you a slut or a man-whore; well not, to your face.

I sit and think about it, and I've said it and really believed that I meant it *4* times (4 isn't that bad!? Right?) But I look back on it now, and that can't be right. How in the hell could I have loved 4 different people at 4 different times in my life (pretty sure they were all different times.) If the meaning of life as I described it is to love, then how could I have truly loved 4 different women in my life? Does love as the meaning of life, really mean to Love as many and as often as possible? I don't believe so, I think that it means find true love once, embrace it and hold on as tight as you can. One life, one love you could say.

So now I'm sure you're asking "Mitch well what about the others? What about the other times you said you loved?" This is where it becomes complicated I think. Where some people might just stop reading this all together. I don't mean to insult anyone but it's rather simple, it just wasn't love before. It was something else, what you ask? I'm not sure there is a label for it. Allow me to give you my quick definition of love to possibly help understand it better.

Love—A BONDING emotion between TWO people. That tells you that you can't live without the other person. (Have you ever see those pictures of twins born attached to each other? That's love, only you're connected spiritually and emotionally.) You hurt when they cry and it really hurts. You laugh when they laugh even if you have no idea at all what the hell is so funny. The cure for all ills and wrongs, the cares, the sorrows and the crimes of humanity, all lies in the one word 'love'. It is the divine vitality that everywhere produces and restores life.

Love is an emotion that takes two people. It can't be one sided or it's something else all together. Maybe a cool new word that hasn't even been thought up yet; stalker fits for some situations. The fact of it is, if those other relationships in my life had been love they never would have ended.

True love, you've got one shot at it, with one person. If not with them, you might as well become that old guy or girl at the bar that everyone is looking at and wondering what the hell is wrong with you. You know the one that I'm talking about.

Please don't confuse or misunderstand me, love isn't easy. I like to think of it like this; I'm sure you've all heard the expression "Shit Happens!" Well this is one of the most incorrect statements ever. Shit doesn't just happen, shit takes time, shit takes effort. Think about the whole process. I doubt you need me to go in to details, but it starts with eating and after many hours the food you consumed exits the body. It's a process where a long chain of events causes one outcome. Look at love the same way it's just not as dirty, well for most of us at least. *Love takes time! Love takes effort!*

To be clear, I do not believe in that whole "fate" scenario where there are two people destined to be with each other. I do believe that we only find real love once, and hopefully we are smart enough to recognize it and hold on to it with all our might. I don't like the idea of there being a soul mate picked out ahead of time, because that makes me feel like I'm not in control of my own life. That is not a feeling I like, I like to know that every aspect of my life is my choice, from the underwear I pick out in the morning, (if I choose to wear any at all) to love. I am in control of my own life, as are each of you.

My definition of love may not fit for you, we are all different people and our emotions react differently. So come up with your own understanding of the emotion, but make sure it's your own; you can't love using someone else's meaning.

I'M KIND OF A BIG DEAL

Before we dig in to the ideas and stories that I want to share, I think it's really important to spend a little time talking about you. Yeah that's right, let's talk about you. Obviously I'm not really there so you'll do most of the talking I'm afraid. Unless you have somehow trapped me in some elevator or some other inescapable situation, or, of course, if you're a friend. We are going to talk about you, because you are the most important thing going on in your life.

When I say let's talk about you, I want to talk about how you perceive yourself, what you see when you look in the mirror. All or at least most of us, at some point, have said, "What's wrong with me?" after being dumped or rejected by someone. Hell, I've said it myself before (I know that's hard to believe for those who know me, but it's true.) It's garbage; there isn't a worse statement out there. From this moment on, that phrase is like a swear word, it's actually four swear words. It's a copout and I will have none of it, and neither will you! It's not what's wrong with me; it's what's wrong with them!

Do you know why the Star High school jock always has a hot girlfriend no matter what he looks like? Because he walks around thinking he has the biggest penis on the planet and he believes it so much that everyone else falls for it as well. Why does the head cheerleader always have guys drooling over her? Because she walks around thinking she's the prettiest thing on this planet and people seem to play along. He probably has a small penis and she without question has an eating disorder. The fact is that they believe in themselves. No one finds depressed people attractive. Those people radiate confidence, they believe in who they are and what they do. That's where you need to be if you want to be successful, not just in relationships but also in life.

Take me for example; I've never been the best-looking guy in the crowd—average looks at best. I have a small penis and I know it (though it is very cute) and I was never a cheerleader, let alone the head cheerleader—lord knows I tried my best. Regardless of my flaws, I've always had my choice of ladies. Why? Because I'm confident—hell truthfully, I'm borderline conceited. The point I'm trying to make is that whether you're the Jock with the giant cock or the Class Nerd, you are beautiful. Ok, ok so that sounded really corny and I'm sorry. What I meant to say is that you have something to offer. Yeah, I'm talking about you. Have you ever seen that movie Revenge of the Nerds? Classic example of what I'm talking about, in the end the Nerd gets the Cheerleader— why? Certainly not because he's good at astrophysics, no it's because he knew he had something to offer. She just needed to take a second to see it and he didn't go away until she noticed it.

Confidence beams from people, I walk in to a room and people turn to look, not because I'm great looking or that I'm someone important. No they look because I give off the vibe that I'm a big deal. It's not even an act with me, I kind of am a big deal. Why, you might ask? Because I have something to offer. I was bartending once and a buddy of mine came in with a date—she was Canadian, but still cute (as far as Canadians go, know what I mean.) She started paying a lot of attention to me. My friend noticed and asked her what it was that I had that he didn't. I'll never forget what she said:

16

"Because there is something about him. He's mysteriously confident. I just want to know more about him, I can't help it. He acts like he can have any girl he wants in here, while you act like you're lucky to even be out with a girl."

That blew me away, him too I think. But right then and there things kind of clicked for me. I realized that you have to know, trust and believe in yourself and what you have to offer to people. The girls want the Alpha male and that has nothing to do with who can kick who's ass.

It applies to the ladies as well; guys aren't interested in some girl who acts like she's a nobody. Everyone has something to offer, regardless of the physical stuff; short, tall, fat, skinny, white, black, gay or straight——you have something to offer. You need to pound that in to your brain, say it in the mirror if you have to.

Okay, so I said this Chapter would be about you, and what I have done but talk about myself the whole time. But ask yourself this, what do I have to offer, what's great about me? Seriously, forget about the physical stuff, sex can be bought in just about every town in the world. Think about what makes you different, why do your friends like you? That's a good place to start. Why did your ex like you? Don't be afraid to ask, it's good to know— Why me?

Another phrase or word I really dislike is 'Can't'. It's just another copout. My favorite is the guy who says "I can't go over and talk to a girl like that!" To that guy I reply, "Then you'll never have a girl like that!" A true story that has nothing to do with relationships but a good bit about confidence. Late in a basketball game when I young, my coach drew up a play for me to take the last shot. A game winning shot in a rec basketball game seems meaningless when you're older but I assure you when I was 12 it was life or death. He drew up the play, and the first words from my mouth were "Coach, I can't make that shot." He put his clipboard down and told me that if I didn't believe I could make it, I never would. He tried boosting my confidence and got me to the point that I told him I thought I could do it. So the time comes, and I take the shot, and what do you know, I missed the thing and missed it bad. After the game, my coach asked me if I knew why we lost that game. I told him that I should have passed the ball and let someone else take the shot. He replied:

"Well, you'll miss every one of those shots son; you have no chance of making a shot you never take. Problem is you never believed you could make that shot."

He was right I didn't. Right now you're saying to yourself— 'What the hell does you choking in a Pee Wee basketball game have to do with love and relationships?' What it has to do with it is confidence—you have to believe in you and believe in you enough to take that chance. There is no person who is out of your league.

Confidence is the key, know yourself, trust yourself, and realize that you have something to offer. You are unique, each and every one of us is, but it's the ones who utilize that trait who get to where they want to go in life.

THE ERVIN FACTOR

I have this friend who I've been friends with as long as I can remember. Maybe the nicest all around guy I've ever met in my life. But the guy has no luck at all, none what so ever. By the time he was age ten a car had hit him—twice, by the same lady nonetheless. This isn't going to be about his accidents as a child or even about how friend and former boss paid a semi handicapped woman $10 to chase him around until she could grab hold of his balls. We won't talk about why he was covered in baby oil while wearing a bridesmaid's gown or the time there was talk of a fight and his nose began to bleed, causing the security guard to ask "Who did this to you?" No this is going to be about Ervin (which is not his name but it is what we will call him because he seems a bit scared to see his name in print), and the worst luck any man on this planet has ever had with women.

It's been said that nice guys finish last, and Ervin himself defines that statement. To prove my point I'm going to let you in on a few situations that Ervin has gone through. Let's start with something recent to show that this is an ongoing extravaganza for him. He recently gave online dating a shot, thought he'd give meeting women online a try. You figure you build a good relationship up front and it's based a lot less on the physical attributes of a person. So after some emailing back and forth, and maybe a few phone conversations they agree to go out to dinner. After a $215 dinner (which in southern Maine is rather hard to do) he hasn't heard from her since. And knowing Ervin, he ordered conservatively, so as to not look like a pig. $215 for a few emails and an hour of her time, I guess cheap isn't a prefix he can use when he tells everyone that she's a whore.

We'll travel back in time a little for this next example. Back to a time when he was dating a girl who we'll call Beca, again just to have a name to relate the story to. I recall this situation, she was a coworker of his and it took him a while to convince her to go out with him. They dated for a little while and things seemed to be going well. One night they are playing a little game called "just the tip" in his drive way of all places—funny what a little making out can turn in to. I wasn't there so I don't have a ton of specifics, but someone's ass hit the horn, it could have been hers, his or the blow up doll, no one will ever really know for certain. The horns no big deal though really, right? Well if you live at home with your parents, as he did, and your dad comes outside in his underwear, as his did and tells you to "Get your fucking ass inside!" As his dad did. (That is a direct quote by the way). I'm not sure if the pun was intended or not, like I said I wasn't there. I hate to laugh at the events he has been through, but what his dad said given the situation is funny as hell.

I could go on for hours, I really could, I could talk about the time his girlfriend zipped up his man hood after her mom caught her practicing a little fellatio. Those are three stitches you don't brag about. Or the time when he had to explain to U.S. Customs why his khaki shorts were covered in blood as he was bringing his Canadian girlfriend home. They accused him of hitting her, while I will use the word '*hit*' very loosely here, hit it he certainly did, but I am certain there was no fist involved. I could get in to all the girlfriends he's had that have slept with his friends, or the girls he wanted to date that his friends slept with, but I won't.

This last story is so unreal that if I had not seen it for myself, I never would have believed it. Ervin dated this girl who we will call Heather just to put a name to her. Heather was a very pretty girl, but very quiet as I remember her. Ervin and Heather met his freshman year of college. I'd never seen him as happy as he was when he talked about her, you could tell she was something special to him. A big thing for Ervin was to invite her to his Grandparents 50th wedding anniversary. She accepted and, I will add looked fabulous. The details at this point start to become a little vague because I was told the rest of the story from a highly intoxicated Ervin who I later had to carry back across the Canadian bridge in to the United States. It appears that Heather kind of hit it off with a cousin of Ervin's. While Ervin was dropping his cousin off at his apartment on the ride home Miss Heather decides she wants to hang out with his cousin. That night she engaged in sexual relations with this cousin, I guess the wedding anniversary was really emotionally moving for her. Here is the punch line on that; Ervin had yet to touch first base. That's right, Ervin can't seem to put the ball in play with her after months of work, and his cousin pinch-hits and knocks it out of the park on the first pitch. Needless to say they're relationship didn't last much longer. Not long after it was finally over, it was discovered that Heather had a liking for girls. She has since been banished to Whore Island.

The stories could go on they seriously could, but I want to make sure I state a semi-serious point here. Ervin is one of the nicest guys I have ever met in my life; he is one of those guys that will do anything for his Girlfriend, and I mean anything. Sadly, women have just walked all over him his entire life. They have used him for whatever they needed and moved on, wiping their feet with him on their way out the door. Just last weekend, he was talking to a girl at the bar and she left him there to go stand in the corner by herself. What kind of girl treats a guy or any human being like that? Well, let me tell you, those are the only kind of girls he seems to find.

Here is the serious point I want to make; even after the hell Ervin has been through, his head is still up, he is still smiling. When I asked him how he can still smile he said, "Life is too short" and he is right. I have never met a person with a more positive outlook on life, he's always about having a good time, no matter how many times he's been kicked to the ground. If everyone could take his outlook on life, there would be a lot less problems in this world.

The Ervin Factor—Getting up and smiling no matter how many times you've had your heart broken and penis stitched up.

He may be the nicest guy on the planet and he can't land a good girl in a serious relationship, what is wrong with this picture? Do nice guys really finish last? Nice Girls don't finish last no they end up happily married with 3 kids, a minivan and a big ass rock on their hand. But why, why is it so different for guys and girls? I've been doing a lot of thinking about this, (and to be honest I was drinking while I was doing this thinking, clearly improving the whole thought process tenfold) and I think I have come to understand what it is about nice guys that can't get them the girl they want.

Most people have accepted that nice guys don't land the girl because they are too nice thus ending up in the ever dreaded friend zone (which isn't as bad as people make it out to be). I don't find that statement to be true. Not that it couldn't be so, but I just don't want to believe women are that blind. How could a girl not see that a guy is being nice to her to gain some sort of upper hand romantically? Girls think about it, how many guys have you met, that are really nice and come with no strings attached? Seriously now, you can tell when a guy is interested in you, hell we make it obvious enough most of the time.

Here is my theory. This is not an attack on my friend Ervin because I honestly love the kid. I think if ladies would get out of their own way long enough to see what kind of guys are really out there and what he had to offer, he'd be considered a real catch. (This really doesn't apply to him because he is a genuine nice guy, the rarest type, a one in ten million type.) Nice guys are needy, almost selfish. Seems a little contradicting doesn't it, but think about it like this. Nice guys are overly nice because they want to gain everyone's approval and be accepted socially. So they go out of their way to please you, but who are they really pleasing? Maybe it's that they are pleasing their own need to be accepted. Nice guys need the people around them to think highly of them or they can't think highly of themselves. They are really dependent people.

Nice guys feel like you owe them something. They have been so nice to you so you should in return do what they want. So their thought process breaks down like this; *Be overly nice to her and gain her approval and trust. After a little while, she will realize how nice I am and everything I do for her ands he will have no choice but to give me a chance and go out with me.* Sounds kind of creepy doesn't it? But looking at it from that perspective I can start to understand why women don't go for the nice guy. A guy who believes in himself, and realizes that he has something that someone is going to want, doesn't have to be overly nice or shower that person with gifts just to get her attention.

Don't get me wrong, there are some honest and real genuine nice guys out there who bring nothing but positive energy in to everyone's life. But for the most part the nice guys of the world have an agenda, a list of demands if you will, and they'll hold you emotionally hostage until they get what they want.

My advice to the nice guys of the world, stop faking it, you're ruining it for the legitimate nice guys. Nobody likes a poser, so stop trying to use a rare quality to take advantage of women. You sit and wonder why you never get the girl, and it's because after a certain time your true self is going to shine through no matter how much makeup you use to disguise it. It's going to come out sooner or later, you might as well be up front about it. If you like a girl and want to be romantically involved with her, make it obvious and well known. Don't become her doormat or her little bitch, have some self respect.

To the ladies I say this, there really are some unbelievably great guys out there who are unrealistically nice. You need to see things for what they are. Think about it, is this guy taking you out to dinner, buying you anything you want and sending you flowers once a week because he wants to be your friend? Chances are unlikely. I'm not saying it doesn't and can't happen. I'm saying that you need to play the numbers here. If he acts like that or seems so incredibly nice for a guy friend then you need to consider the possibility that he's interested in being more than just your friend, and you need to address it. You not saying anything can trigger one of the most dangerous things in a situation like that, and that is for a guys mind to start assuming things (and I assure you that the guy always assumes in his favor).

My words of wisdom to Ervin are to keep his head up and just keep being who you are, my friend. You have such a great outlook on life and some great girl is going to realize that one day, and you'll never have to look for another chic again in your life! (For all you single ladies out there looking for a great all around guy, don't hesitate to send a little fan mail, I'll see that he gets it!)

DO YOU COME HERE OFTEN?

Meeting the right person can be a challenge for anyone. There is nothing wrong with being picky, nothing wrong with it at all. We are talking about love and relationships here not what toppings you want on your pizza. It's actually good to be picky, to a certain extent. You don't want to be so picky that you're holding out for Brad Pitt or Angelina Jolie (I had initially wrote Brittany Spears hear, but she doesn't have any hair now so it just didn't feel right.). Most people's issue isn't actually about being picky, even though that is the excuse that they use. No, the issue is that they are looking in the wrong places.

Think about it for a second ok. Say you're hunting for crocodiles (God bless the Crock Hunter (RIP) and Animal Planet.); you won't go looking for them in some small pond in the Allagash (which is in very, very northern Maine for those of you who don't know.) Lord knows there are many things in the Allagash, but I doubt that you'll find any crocks. No, you'd go to Mississippi or somewhere else in the southern hemisphere and search a swamp. You don't go to McDonalds for a T-bone steak do you? No! So why look for love in places that doesn't fit for you?

I really hate to break things down to a male and female kind of thing but it must be done for this topic. Guys, the worst place you can go looking for women, is just about your favorite place on the planet—the strip club. Come on now, how many respectable women are you going to drag out of there? None that you'd want to take home to your parents. (Well maybe Dad, but it was his dirty magazines that got your interests peaked to begin with.) I'm not saying avoid the strip club, by all means no, that would be inhumane. But if the only life you have outside of work and watching your porn is to go to the strip club, then it is kind of an issue.

Ladies, it is a bit different for you since the guy is usually the one chasing after you. Hell it should be easy for you, guys come to you and you can just weed your way through them. You can try out the guys that interest you and just ignore the rest of them. WRONG! If you want something in life go and get it, damn it! The times have changed. It is now socially acceptable for you to go talk to a guy first. Most guys would be flattered if some girl came up and hit on him. Hell I am when it happens. It happened to me when I was in Boston visiting a friend. I'm just sitting there at The Tap (A Great Bar, in the historic Faneuil Hall on Union St.), complaining about how bad the Boston Celtics have gotten and out of nowhere comes this attractive girl. Well I was talking about the Celtics so I was drinking a lot, she really could have been a man for all I know, but that's not the point right now. She comes over and just introduces herself. I bought her a drink for the simple fact that she came up to me. Guys find it flattering, and worst case, you can drink all night for free, (well, if you run in to me at the bar you certainly can!).

The best place to meet someone compatible, is somewhere of interest and comfort to you. Some place that you have to be for a reason other then "picking up chics" or "Meeting Mr. Right." The first place that came to your mind was the supermarket wasn't it? That can work, but it's honestly not what I had in mind. I'm thinking more of a place that interests you. Maybe a a place while practice a hobby or a place you go to cheer for your favorite sports team. Maybe you're in karate class or work out at local gym or go to the same bar every Sunday to watch your favorite football team play.

Meeting someone in a place of your interest puts you ahead of the game. You already have something to talk about, a common interest. It also takes some pressure off. Why? Because you didn't go there to meet them, you were there and happened to form an interest in them. You have to work a little harder at the Club or a Supermarket. You're starting from scratch, unless you want to use the good ole line "Do you come here often?" Maybe that line works for you; it's just not my style. At the Supermarket you could be like "Nice piece of meat you have there!" but that just sounds to dirty. I'm not trying too say that you can't meet someone in a club or in the supermarket, but why make it harder on yourself?

If you insist on meeting someone at a club, here are some basic things to keep in mind that can help improve your chances.

First you always want to travel with friends, but never too many of them. I'd keep it under 5 and closer to 3 if you can. The reason being simply this; girls in large groups can be very intimidating for a guy. Picture this; there is a girl out with ten of her closest friends. I find her attractive from across the room. Now whether I have the bartender bring her a drink, or I walk it over there myself, at some point I still need to walk over there and talk to her. Or I just wasted $10 buying her a drink. Eleven girls all in one group may sound like a fantasy all guys would love, but in this situation it's hell. It's like a gauntlet for a guy; he's walking over, being judged by each and every one of them. Does he want to date or even talk to all eleven of them? Doubtful (though I am always up for a challenge, I was told once I do a really good job of balancing the conversation and keeping everyone involved. It was only 2 girls that night though), but they will still judge and will most definitely talk about him when he's gone. That could scare a guy off, and boom you both lose out. So I'd advise to keep the groups smaller.

The second part of being with your friends is that, believe it or not your friends know you and your taste. Guys almost always get the approval of at least one of their friends before they make the journey across the bar to talk to a girl. And girls like I said, will judge and talk about a guy—god forbid your shoes don't go with your outfit. Trust your friends to an extent, especially if they have had a bit less to drink than you have. They can save you from making a very big mistake. (Jason I can't ever thank you enough, her hands were bigger then my head.)

I have friends that often ask me what pickup lines I use, and which ones are most effective. The truth is that I don't use them and I don't think they work. They could work if they were used properly, but the guy often makes up his mind on what he's going to say long before he is ever close enough to make a true assessment of the female. He'll go up to her and tell her she has beautiful eyes, long before he can ever actually see them. You'd have much better luck saying "That outfit would look fantastic crumpled up on my floor in the morning." Pickup lines are meant to be a sweet, short statement to kind of sweep the girl off her feet. Over time they have become so terribly corny that they are just used for humor now.

The most effective way to pick someone up at a bar or a club is to use basic conversation. "Hi my name is…" and then be honest. "I took a bit of an interest in you from across the room and mustered up the courage to come see if I could buy you a drink. I'd like to learn a bit more about you." Then you need to listen to what the other person has to say, and really listen. This will help make for a really smooth transition in to a conversation. This is effective because it's you being you; you're not pretending to be some smooth pimp, throwing out every pick up line that you heard in some movie. Don't go over there to just ask for her number, why would she want to give it to you without knowing anything about you. The objective is to really just lay a small foundation, give her enough information about you and show enough interest in what she has to say for her to give you her phone number. Don't try to get in her pants that night, not if you're looking for a serious and meaningful relationship. (The one-nightstand book will follow this one, and will be much longer, I'm sure.)

Another great way to meet someone on a romantic level is one of your friends. I'm not talking about having your friend hook you up with a friend of theirs, that would be a blind date and that's just a waste of time. I'm talking about hooking up with a friend, someone you already know. This saves a ton of time, you don't have to find a common interest. It's your friend for god's sake, you should already have something in common. You should also already have a certain level of trust established. While it won't be the same type of trust you need for a romantic relationship, at least you're not starting from scratch. It sounds simple huh? But it is a very dangerous option. A very big gamble that could end up costing you a lot more in the end than you initially realize.

It is very, very hard to go from friends to lovers and back to friends again. It just doesn't happen often. Trust me I know about this one first hand. This girl that was one of my best friends in high school, who will remain nameless because we no longer speak. Our friendship grew in to something more and it happened really fast without much notice at all, and it ended almost as fast, about two months later. Maybe I've talked to her a total of 5 times since. She's married now and I didn't even get invited to the wedding, but I still wish her the best. The whole situation sucks because we used to talk about everything. I lost that for two months worth of sex basically, it certainly wasn't love. I think you can only really love once, so I guess you can call it lust. But it cost me that friendship and given the chance to do it again, I wouldn't make that gamble; the price was just too high.

Please don't let my troubled past relationships dispirit you. A good friend of mine Jess dated her best friend and things were great for a while. They ended up breaking up but they are now friends again, obviously that took a little time. I asked her if she'd do it the same if given the chance to do it all over again and she said she would without hesitation. So that goes to show you that even if it doesn't work on a romantic level, a strong friendship can prevail in the end. Jess told me that the friendship was strong, and if your friendship is strong enough it can make it through anything.

As I look back at things now and ponder the friendship to relationship scenario. I can't help but wonder 'what if' about a girl I would have considered my best friend in High School. Jenn and I were always together, our lockers were practically next to each other, we were in all the same classes and we had a ton in common. She was the reason I kicked an early drug habit, but that's a whole other book. We were together so much in high school, that my high school girl friend was actually jealous of her. Every time we'd fight she'd bring Jenn up. But that was years ago now, and you can't sit there wondering 'what if?' You have to act on your thoughts, feelings and desires now, so you never find yourself asking 'what if?'.

You really need to understand the risk you could be taking when getting involved with a friend. There is a good chance that if things go bad, they go bad for a while. I'm not saying forever because that's too definite of a word for me. Don't expect to break up on Tuesday and hang out on Friday and everything will go back to the way it was before you tried to take the relationship to the next level. With any big risk comes the chance for a big reward. That friend could really be the love of your life. But is the risk worth the reward?

With the coming of technology and the internet being what it is today, it is only right to drop a little line about meeting someone via the web. Personally, I have always been against the idea; I think there is a certain exchange of body language that is essential when you meet someone. But with there being so many internet dating sites out there, promising you true love in 6 months it's hard not to want to check it out, to find out who is out there that you are missing. I have never done it, never met anyone romantically online, but I'm certainly not knocking it. I've just never done it, so I am in no position to talk negatively about it.

Above all the dating websites with their promises, there is MySpace, which promises nothing on the relationship level but offers you access to more people than you could ever imagine. MySpace itself may be the most addicting website of all time, well, minus that one where you could see naked pictures of me but that's different. My rule with MySpace is simple; I only add the people I know or people that somehow catch my interest right away. That doesn't mean the girls with the naked photos, though I will admit that I do browse those profiles when I get the friends request. I can't hate on MySpace at all, it's an addiction and is also where this whole book began.

Some things to keep in mind when you're searching the web for people to meet on a relationship level. You need to be honest; so many people online just lie, flat out. If it's not in their personal profile they have doctored their photo or it's not even them in the photo at all. You can do unreal things with Photoshop; I put my head on Superman's body—I know that's hot, right. The last thing I'd like to warn about the internet thing is that there are some sick people out there so be careful. That profile that claims to be an 18 year old college freshman girl is really a 55 year old guy who sits around in his boxer shorts and a wife beater all day long, while he uses the 3 day pass on all the porno sites with no intentions what so ever of becoming a member. I don't know, can love have *www* in front of it?

Like I have said before and will say many more times throughout this book, every situation and person is different. I only hope to offer a little bit of information that will help you understand the little things that people often over look about love and relationships.

FIRST DATES
ARE INTERVIEWS

You don't want to be too excited to call him or her after you've met and exchanged numbers. Try to give it at least 24 hours before you make that initial call, but wait longer if you can. The objective is to call before they have forgotten about you, but not so soon that they still remember what you smelled like. For example you meet on Friday evening and call Sunday afternoon. I don't recommend trying to set something up for that day or night; it is to short of notice. And before I dig too deep here, I know it's the age of technology but, actually call, don't text or instant message the person. While these are good tools to learn more about the person and communicate, it's just a little too impersonal for initial contact. (Having said that, I send out an apology to just about every girl I know, I am the king of text messages. But I am single, so that's a clue that you should actually call.)

Before you make that call, you need to do a few things. First check your schedule, you don't want to plan a date for Wednesday night if that's poker night or lunch on Thursday if you planned to spend it with the ladies. Always have a "B" day or a backup day if you will. If Tuesday works best but Thursday works just as well, make the later one (Thursday), The "B" day. You need to have a plan of what you want to do or where you want to go—This has always been an issue for me. I always want to let the lady pick, thinking I'm being nice. But I've found out that women find it attractive if a guy comes ready with a plan.

-What to Do on That First Date-

Dinner and a movie has been thought to be a no fail first date, I tend to disagree. Dinner is great, everyone needs to eat so you really can't go too wrong with dinner. As far as the movie, how much can you learn about a person sitting there in silence for two hours? Not much, unless you are one of those people who talk during movies. In which case expect to get some popcorn thrown at you especially if I'm watching the same movie. Come up with some different ideas. Something fun that will allow the two of you to have a conversation. Go for a walk, mini-golf, museum or a Karaoke bar. Just do something other than dinner and a movie.

First things first, about the restaurant, you need to have some different types of restaurants in mind. Don't just pick some Steak house, have a Chinese and Italian place in mind as well. People are really picky eaters these days, not to mention all the diet fads that make people count points or carbs or each grain of salt. So throw some options at them, see what fits for them. One last word of advice on the restaurant, don't take them to the place you and your EX used to go all the time. Chances are you'll start talking about them, and that's really nothing you want to get in to on the first date.

My recommendation for the ideal first date is lunch in the middle of the week. Why, you might ask? For a few simple reasons that you have probably never thought of. Firstly if you go to lunch there is a time limit on things. Most people have an hour for lunch break, so that means if it's going badly and you figure in travel time, you only have to spend about 30-40 minutes on a bad date. Secondly there is not the added pressure that sex puts on things. The pressure has the guy wondering if he'll score and the girl wondering how long she can put it off so she doesn't seem like a slut. Lunch is kind of like speed dating in the respect that there is a time limit and no added pressure. And if things are going well, it leaves an easy opening for a second date.

-The Objective of the First Date-

First dates are interviews. A chance to feel each other out, and by feel I am not talking about physical touching. Once you've locked down a place and a time. Asking questions and actually listening are very important for different reasons for both the male and the female. For the male it's good because asking questions and listening shows you're interested in more than her body—though don't be afraid to compliment her on her appearance. For the ladies, you asking questions will not only show an interest in the guy, it also helps the guy open up a little. Considering that most guys are a little reserve, and only talk about the simple things life has to offer.

Fellas, keep something in mind; she has already said yes to going out with you when she could have said no. So you don't have to overdo it, don't try too hard to impress her. Don't try to be something you're not. Your job here is not to blow it like we usually do. If you're funny, be funny. She's looking for the real you, even if she doesn't want it all at once. When she's talking look her in the eye and actually listen and then respond. This shows you have an interest in more than her body. If you're nervous say so not everyone can be Casanova. A good friend of mine said to a girl once and I'll never forget, it went like this

Friend: "You know you have a kind chin."
Girl: "A kind chin??"
Friend: "Yeah, the kind of chin I could rest my balls on!"

I won't get in to what happened after that, but that's an example of some of the stupid things guys will do.

Ladies don't feel like you have to try so hard to impress us. You've already impressed us enough for us to ask you out. Just be you, and try not to be so guarded. Relax, smile and enjoy yourself.

What questions to ask, how personal do I get? You only want to scratch the surface on the first date. You should already know some things about them, some basic things at least, after all you did have to talk to them to get their number. Right?!? Unless this is a blind date, in which case you should just cancel it right now. Seriously, do you know anyone that has had a successful blind date? No, I didn't think so. Blind date sex, most certainly. I didn't get all dressed up and take you out for nothing. Good relationships rarely come from such things. Sorry got a little distracted there, back to what questions to ask. Ask what they do for work, and after they answer dig in to that a little. Don't be afraid to ask about what interests and hobbies they have. One of the questions that I try to ask early on, is if they want to make out? Ok don't ever, ever use that one, though I will say it's really effective for me. My personality allows me to play it off as a joke, so they laugh. The objective is to learn enough about them to plan a bit more personal second date.

So the date goes like this, you talk a little, you eat, talk a bit more and maybe drink a little. Try to keep the alcohol consumption under control on that first date. (Trish that wasn't directed at you, I was the one feeding you drinks that night at the Old Port Tavern, my bad.) Some other things to keep in mind, first be yourself, the real you is going to shine through at some point, you might as well get it out of the way right of the back. Don't force things, especially humor; guys do this more than the girls, trying to impress them. If you're funny be funny, by being you. Don't bring out the knock-knock jokes in an attempt to make her laugh. The last thing I would advise is to not spend the whole time talking about you. If a girl tells me everything about her on the first date, she takes all the mystery out of it. We might as well go back to my place rip each others clothes off, hop in the sack, get sweaty then you go home and we don't talk again. Come on now, where is all the fun in that. You want to talk just enough about you so that they can't help but want to go on a second date.

WANNA MAKE OUT

Did you ever see that movie Hitch? Remember when Will Smith (Hitch) says that line about how 8 of 10 women believe they can tell if the relationship is going to work from the first kiss? Well my research didn't yield results as high as 80%, actually a bit closer to 65%. But still 65% is a high number when you think about the subject, a kiss, 65% that's like every two out of three girls.

I'm not going to tell you how to kiss, there is no perfect technique, and everyone likes something different. But some basic pointers are always a bit helpful. The most important thing I can ever share with you about kissing is this, less is more.

Remember when Lays Potato chips dared us that we couldn't eat just one? Know why that was effective? Cause it seems to be human nature to want what we can't have. Someone tells you not to look down, what is the first thing you do? That's right you look down. You must be thinking 'what the hell does this have to do with kissing?' Simply, you want to leave them wanting more. Guys don't try to stretch a single in to a homerun. Don't try to get in her pants on the first kiss. Even if she seems to be allowing it. Pull back a little, take a moment to stare in to her eyes. What happens from there is on you. But Fellas if you pull back it speaks something about you, without you ever saying a word. It lets her know that you respect her and it's not just about sex. Now, if when you pull back, she starts to unbutton your pants, by all means be the perverted teenager your mind wants you to be. After all, the penis is the control center for our body.

Ladies it's kind of different for you. We kind of expect you to pull back (though we do hope you'll undo our pants.) We expect to hear you say 'lets slow down a little'. So don't think we'll call you a tease if you do (well we might to our friends, but that's only because we are insecure and think sex=love and love=sex.) I would rather have a tease than someone who is "easy". Early in a relationship it's all about the chase. Me chasing you trying to get you naked, and you trying to stall me as long as you can. I've heard every excuse there is and I have come backs for most of them, but that's a different time. It all goes back to wanting what we can't have.

You want to get spoiled a little ladies? Just hold out on the sex for a minute. All the guys reading this must hate me right about now, asking whose side I'm on and what not. But trust me here guys that waiting a bit makes it all worth it. Think about it this way if you will, try to recall a time you slept with a girl on the first date or even a girl you just met at the bar. If the sex was great you'd probably call the next day. What if it wasn't great? More to the point, how many of those first niters have turned in to relationships that have lasted longer than three months? I just sat down with some scrap paper and an adding machine and after some serious multiplication and long division this is the number I came up with from my own personal experience—ZERO. I couldn't think of one that lasted more than a few weeks. The longest being 21 days and then a little reminiscing a month or so later when we were both drunk at the bar, but she talked me in to that. The last real relationship I was in, to my surprise the girl didn't throw herself at me, and she held out on me. That made me want her even more, and she made me work for it and you know what? That's what made it so exciting.

I'm getting a head of myself here; this is just about a kiss, not sex. The first kiss really is a special moment. I can honestly tell you where I was (maybe even what I was wearing) when I've kissed every girl that I've ever kissed. Now names are a different story but I never was good with names. People talk about magic or a spark of sorts. Magic is just an illusion and I don't know that I've ever started a fire from kissing but I certainly admit to something. Call it chemistry or a connection, but I've felt something. It's different for everyone but you'll know when that kiss means something more. For me it's when I can't leave. I normally have no problem kissing and leaving. I like to leave them wanting more, but if for some reason that kiss makes me linger around then you've got me hooked sweetheart. Which I might add is not an easy thing to accomplish. That kissing thing has only happened once in my life, or should I say only happened with one person.

Getting past the whole chemistry thing, kissing is the starting point of sex (it's obvious I have a penis, I go from kissing right to sex; the hell with foreplay!). Kissing is the key that opens the door to sex. I have met some very attractive girls who I would consider and 8 or 9 (I don't give 10's) and was turned off when kissing them. I met a girl one night and my friends were drooling over her. Met her playing basketball at the gym, asked her out and she said yes (like there was ever a doubt). We went out a week later, dinner and a movie—Bad Boys II if I'm not mistaken. I had a great time with her, she was fun to be with and on top of that she kept telling me how lucky she was to be out with such a sweet guy. At this point I'm thinking she's a keeper, for a little bit at least. I was living close to the beach at the time so I took her out on the pier to take in the beautiful night (Ok that's a lie I took her there to get her

40

drunk and take advantage of her). It was out on the patio that the moment occurred, you know when there is that silence and that eye contact that screams "shut up and kiss me." So I kissed her and it was over, the attraction was gone. Call me shallow if you want, but there just wasn't anything there. I still talk to her, we're good friends, and I hooked her up with one of my drooling buddies. Get this; he said she was a dynamite kisser, so it proves that we all want something different. They've been together for a few years now.

The most important thing to remember is that less really is more, in the long run. You don't want to rush the kiss; it's really all about timing. I dated a girl who almost didn't want to see me again because by the third date I hadn't made the move to kiss her yet. I finally did it on the third date, as we walked on the beach (what can I say, I like the beach). The timing just wasn't there for me before that.

Here are some other important things to keep in mind about sucking face that first time. The appropriate place to make the move is somewhere semi public. Somewhere out in the open but where you can be alone. Not everyone wants to see the two of you necking. So keep that in mind, her doorstep is classic, or at the car after the club. Guys keep your hands at home, on the small of her back, not on the back of her head, that's too much too fast. Not on her buttocks, again too much too fast. If not on the small of her back try just holding both of her hands. Pull her in a little but just keep a hold of her hands. This shows respect in a subconscious way. You're not groping her, but holding her hand is still a really intimate act.

I'm no expert on kissing, though I do make out with my mirror on a daily basis, and have yet to hear a complaint from it. I've done research, I've sat and watched (not in a sick touching myself stalker kind of way), you can just tell when two people lock up in that first kiss. There is always that moment after with solid eye contact, (enjoy it ladies our eyes will probably never make it much past your breasts again.) followed with the smile.

There is no right or wrong way to kiss, but as far as the first one here are some basic tips.

Guys

-Breath, my good man. No cigarette or beer breath—even though I do know a few girls who seem to like beer breath. (Women are so weird.) Gum, mints, breath strips—something!

-Don't push it too far

-Don't rush to make it happen. It's all about timing

-No groping

-Most certainly look her in the eyes before and after.

-Don't ruin the moment by talking

-Important, don't ever, ever, ever, ever wipe your mouth right after. This will make her insecure.

Ladies

-Breath

-Don't let it get to far

-Don't get upset if our timing sucks, hell we are a little nervous here

-Don't be afraid of a little contact, there is nothing in our pocket, we're just happy to see you.

-Don't be afraid to express your approval. A hug, smile, or hell a tap on the ass followed by a "good game kid" anything to let us know it was worth it to you.

Just a little side note, ladies, and this is totally situational and about your comfort level with yourself. Don't be afraid to make the first move. Guys believe it or not get nervous as hell about that first kiss. We have hundreds of questions running through our minds. Is it the right time? Does she even want to? Tongue or no tongue? What if I suck at it? Help put those questions to rest ladies. A woman will steal my heart if she ever just throws me up against the wall and plants one on me as the first kiss. It's happened before but just never as that first kiss.

TRUST ME

Trust—assured reliance on the character, ability, strength, or truth of someone or something.
—The Dictionary

My philosophy on trust is rather simple. From day one you get 100% of my trust, until you give me a reason to take it away. It can be a serious fault, and I admit that. Especially if you come home early from a business trip, don't call the girl friend of 6 months and just plan to surprise her with lunch. Oh, she's surprised, as she answers the door in her bathrobe and her X-boyfriend (or should I call him boyfriend number 1. He gets to be number one because technically he was there first) is sitting on the couch in his boxer shorts. That isn't a slap to the face, that's a kick to the balls with those really pointy shoes that girls used to wear when I was in 3rd and 4th grade. But this isn't really about me; she was a pirate hooker anyway. But you need to be really careful with your trust.

It's one thing to be careful, and it's another to be ignorant. It is in no way right to not trust me because your last boyfriend cheated on you. You can't punish me for his crimes. I know it sucks to have been in a bad relationship, trust me I've put many girls through hell so I know. But let's take a second to think about this here, he cheated on you and I get punished. So next time I get insanely drunk you will be sick and hung over for me the next

44

day? Or how about I blame you for the OJ Simpson murders? Or the fact that I was once a New Kids on the Block fan. It doesn't make sense for me to blame you for any of those things does it? No, so how could it make sense for you to punish me for him cheating, I'm not the one who put his tongue in her mouth.(Except for that one time, but the girl was really hot and her boyfriend was a real asshole anyway.)

Trust ties in to every aspect of the relationship, from sex to picking where we go out to eat. You have to have trust. With little help I could write a whole book about trust itself, but I'm going to keep it to a limit here as to not bore the hell out of you. When it comes to relationships, trust has a few stages which will progress as the relationship does.

Stage one—The first 24 hours to 7 days. At this point he or she may know very little about you. So the trust level is very low, but it's not nonexistent. Right now it's about the basics, name, occupation, age, ("I never said I was 28, everyone else did and you never asked. What's 2 years really, when we like each other, right?!") and your current dating status. You'd be surprised how many people lie about this, guys and girls alike. You're laying the foundation here; you need them to be able to trust you, now and down the road. So I'd advise against using the French Exchange student game to pick her up. (Jason, I still can't believe she knew French that whole time and waited so long to bust us.) They don't want the whole you just yet, so don't put it all out there. Trust them enough so you can be honest with them and vice-versa. Trust, like love, is a mutual thing, if it's not a two way thing then you've got nothing.

Quick story, I know all these damn stories but, it fits well for the early stage of a relationship. I'd just started dating this girl. We'd both taken a little break since our last relationships. Her past relationship was a bit more serious than mine, but who is comparing here, I'm still cute. Part of my personality makes me a very flirtatious person by nature. It's harmless and is for nothing more than to see someone smile. Growing up the majority of my friends were girls as well, so I flirt by nature and don't even notice it. My new girlfriend would get upset, though she never said a word. Until one night, The Captain (Captain Morgan) pushed me overboard, I had a bit much to drink and my flirty personality ran wild. We were at a local club that I often frequented. I knew almost everyone there, hell, my name was on the girl's bathroom wall and I didn't even have to write it myself this time. So to say I was a regular would have been an understatement. Anyway, from what little I remember and what I've been told, there were ladies all over me all night long. The girlfriend got pissed, but didn't say anything to me. Oh no she says it to her friend, who comes over to me and says. "So and So (no names) is pissed at you." And I reply confidently "She'll get over it (dramatic pause), they always do." That line cost me a few trust points there. I threw up, blacked out and had my meatball sub stolen from me while I was photographed hugging the toilet. There is a point to this, I swear. I had no idea about the whole flirting thing, does that make it right? Most definitely not, but the thing was that she never bothered to tell me it was an issue. Her last boyfriend had cheated, and I knew that, but honestly how is that my fault, right? The point is the communication wasn't there. Maybe she didn't trust me enough to say, "Hey that bothers me." Or maybe she was just afraid it would scare me off, who knows for sure. But after some time, a little begging, some expensive gifts (that she later returned to me), and a few naked Polaroid's of me, we were able to work things out. Obviously not for a long time, because I am single.

In the early stage it's vital to build as much trust as possible for the long run of things. Put things out there honestly, if something bothers you say so. Trust that person enough to let them see the

46

real you. You have to be willing to take a chance on someone once in a while. If not, what's always been, will always be.

Stage two is what I like to call the honeymoon weeks. This is from week one up to month six. Trust takes on a whole new role here, maybe the biggest role it ever plays in a growing relationship. You're still in the starting stage of the relationship, where everything is still great. Maybe you've had a fight or two but nothing too serious. Maybe the Love words have even been uttered (as long as you don't do it in a text message or at a loud club on New Year's Eve, I'm not going to complain about it.) But how much do you really trust them? Would you let them go away for a weekend with their friends and not call them 50 times to 'check in'? Do you trust them enough to move in together? Trust them enough to have sex with them? Or try something new from the pages of the Karma Sutra? Trust them enough that the one attractive person that they work with doesn't bother you? Does he trust you enough for you to tell him that his cooking sucks? Does she trust you enough for you to tell her that those jeans make her ass look big?

The questions could go on and on, the point being that you might not trust them as much as you think. For me, if I love someone I trust them with my life. Ask yourself these questions—someone gives you 5 minutes to make a decision. Five minutes right now to make a decision. Could you spend the rest of your life with the person you're with right now. Clocks ticking…

4 minutes It's just a question right? You care about them, right?

3 minutes Things have gone well so far haven't they? You've never been happier right?

2 minutes Your friends like them, that is good, isn't it? Mom and Dad think they are great, can't go wrong could you?

1 minute You trust them don't you?

30 seconds Rest of your life, that could be a long time couldn't it?

15 seconds We're still attractive to each other aren't we?

10 seconds This is stupid the answer is yes or I wouldn't have wasted this much of my life with them, right?

5 seconds YES!

4 seconds I think so

3 seconds Maybe

2 seconds I'm not sure

1 second I...I...I just need more time!

Thank god that's not how it really works in life. But it served its purpose; you just did a full assessment of your relationship in 5 minutes. It's amazing what a little pressure can do to someone. What do you do now? Certainly do not, I repeat DO NOT start to doubt the other person. What you need to do is talk to them, communication is the key to trust. Communication is vastly important to a relationship. I'll get in to that a bit more later, but without communication you can't have trust, without trust you can't have love.

At this point in the relationship trust is what will make or break things. I wish I had a good story to tell, but like I've stated I'm single. You have to be able to trust the person enough to move on with your life together. This has nothing to do with marriage or even moving in together. It's about knowing them well enough and realizing that it's worth it to take a chance at making it work in the long run. There is still no guarantee that things will work out, relationships are a gamble from start to finish. But trust in yourself enough to take the gamble even if you've lost big before.

Stage three I like to call happily ever after, which can start as early as six months. Since there is no timetable on love this is the last stage of trust. You should both be comfortable with each other. Maybe you're living together, maybe you're not. Maybe you're engaged, maybe your not. Maybe you're just happy with the way things are. At this point you should trust the person a great deal. If not, then you need to seriously evaluate this relationship. If after six months to a year you don't trust them to go out and have a drink with their friends, and they have never given you a reason not to trust them, then there is something seriously wrong.

Depending on you and your partner's age, at this point the odds are finally starting to shift in your favor. Things have been good thus far so they should continue that way correct? Only if you keep working at it, there is always room for improvement. Don't become content with the way things are, always reach for higher but reach together.

Most relationships that burn out early are because of a lack of trust. She thinks he'll cheat so she suffocates him, and keeps a leash on him around the clock. He thinks she'll cheat so he becomes the crazy stalker boyfriend. Relationships become successful when you trust the other person to have their own life, their own friends. It is definitely needed in the early stages of the relationship; you don't need to be together 24/7 even if you want to be. You always need to have some "Me" time, whether it's with your friends or by yourself. It just needs to be your own personal time.

Having your own life does not mean having two or three relationships going at a time. It means maintaining the life you had before you met your new love. It's important for you to have that time, not only to gain trust from the other person but you'll find being away from them can make you really appreciate them. And when you appreciate people you tend not to take them for granted.

COME AND TALK TO ME

A lot of things go in to making a relationship work. I believe the second most important thing to be communication. Communication, or the lack of it, causes more problems than anything else in relationships. Communication is much more than just talking, and has to do with more than just the two of you. It is actually a rather complex subject with certain areas pertaining to the fellas and others pertaining to the ladies.

Guys, the first thing to realize and understand is that women have a very complex mind, they often over think things. For example, say you're walking in the mall and you don't make any attempt to hold her hand or put an arm around her. Her mind starts to process hundreds of questions. She's thinking that maybe you're ashamed of her, or don't want people to know you have a girlfriend. Those questions trigger another hundred or so questions, and you haven't said a word. By not holding her hand it communicated to her through your body language. Her mind makes some observations and assumptions.

Most women automatically assume all guys are perverted pigs. A story to support that theory; I'm stuck in some slow moving traffic with a girlfriend——she's driving. I turn to one side to crack my back, then to the other. She assumes that the cracking the back thing is just a ploy so I can check out the ass of some girl jogging.

Certainly not the case, I didn't even notice the girl running until she accused me. When she confronts me, I kind of laugh because I find humor in it, and we actually had an argument about it. No matter what I said she couldn't seem to understand that I really wasn't checking the other girl out. It happened another time in the mall, I turned over my shoulder to look back at pair of shoes on display at Footlocker and she freaks out again. Ladies, give the guy the benefit of the doubt unless he's given you a reason not to. Fellas don't be afraid to show your lady off in public, hold her hand proud——this is your princess.

Ladies, something to realize, guys for the most part don't think the same way as you. We kind of have simple minds when it comes to that type of communication. For example, if you're mad say something, don't give us the silent treatment, we are not mind readers. We need you to tell us what is wrong, especially if we ask you like 50 times. Because of the way our minds work, we start to try to remember something we've done wrong to cause the mood you're in. If I did something, I want to know so that I can defend myself or correct the issue. Most of the time we, as guys, don't even realize what it is we've done you consider wrong.

Guys for the most part women have no problem sharing their emotions and feelings——but you need to let them know its ok. Some girls will hold back because too much emotion is said to scare guys off. It's certainly not the case, it's just at times we don't know how to reciprocate or respond properly. You need to tell them that very thing, don't just let things go unspoken. The worst thing you can ever say is nothing at all. If you encourage her to share her feelings and thoughts, I guarantee the relationship will be so much stronger. The benefits will extend to all parts of the relationship, the bedroom included guys.

Ladies it's a little more complicated with guys. Often times we don't know how to identify our own emotions, and so we choose to remain silent. You have to help us open up a little, ask questions and don't settle for a bullshit answer. At times it seems that the only feeling a guy knows is when his penis gets hard. Horrifically incorrect, we just lack the knowledge to vocalize our emotions. From the guys I interviewed before writing this book, most admitted to feeling and wanting to tell the girl that they loved her weeks and sometimes months before it was actually ever spoken—they just didn't know how.

The most commonly known aspect of communication is the simple act of talking. You need to be honest and open with each other about things. Don't get me wrong, there are always things you have the right to keep private. But if you want to have a strong bond you need to be able to talk to each other openly and truthfully. That is where a lot of trust comes from. Tell each other when things the other person does bother you. Explain why and offer up a solution to the problem, and by solution I don't mean demanding that they change. I mean offer a compromise, something that works for both of you, and a common ground that can allow you both to be happy.

So many relationships go bad because people don't talk about the important issues. They keep it all bottled up hoping it'll fix itself or just go away. I'm guilty of it myself, I'm a bottler, I keep things to myself, and then when I finally break it all comes out at once. Things from months ago that have long since been forgotten by the other person all comes out at once. That is really bad communication; you could actually describe it as no communication at all. Funny all these things are starting to come together to make me realize why I am single.

There will come a time in every relationship that you will disagree about something. It's expected, hell you can't agree on everything all the time, and if you do, well, you make me sick. But seriously every good relationship has its share of good fights. You really can't agree on everything and if you do it's because one of you is lying and just setting your own personal feelings aside. I'll admit I don't like to fight with a girlfriend; I just hate the emotional roller coaster it sends you on. I will say that fighting can and is very beneficial to a healthy relationship. To be clear, when I talk about fighting, I speak only of a verbal disagreement. I'm not talking of physically hitting anyone or verbally degrading anyone.

The most important thing to come from fighting other then the makeup sex is that you are communicating. Your fight itself might be from a lack of communication, but if you're fighting you are now communicating. You are getting things off your chest, things that are bothering you. The important thing for you is to get your point across, make it known why you feel the way you do. Explain how it makes you feel, try to avoid saying, "Just because it does." Kind of sounds stupid to read it like that doesn't it? Well it sounds just as stupid when you give it as a reason for something upsetting you. You want to be as open as possible here, not only is it going to help you feel better, but it will make it easier to come up with a resolution to the issue.

When it comes to fights, most people get a little selfish, they forget that the other person has feelings as well. Not only does that person have feelings, they have feelings for you and vice versa. So don't make it a personal attack, get your point across and keep it focused on the specific issue at hand. If you turn this in to an assault of their personality you are setting yourself up for trouble. I had an old girlfriend who believed that when we argued she had to try and put me down. That it had to be about more than just the situation. This is how it would play out; we'd start arguing about something, then she would make a personal attack on me. Something about me having bad hair or something. I couldn't just let her walk all over me like that so I'd have to defend myself and comment on her small breasts or fat ass. I didn't want to make it personal, but I had to defend myself. Ok so that whole situation was a lie, I don't have any good fight stories because I don't really like to fight (and like hell any girl would say I have bad hair). That should tell you how important it is, if I don't do it—it needs to be done.

The best part of fighting is clearly making up. I don't need to go in to the details of the makeup sex but I will say a few things. The reason people fight is because they are unhappy with things, fighting gives you a chance to put it out there. It's important for you to be honest with yourself and the other person and don't be afraid to admit you've made a mistake. "Honey I know I messed up, I'm really going to try harder! Can we get naked now or what?"

Communication is so important whether you are fighting or curling up under the stars. This is when you need to be you, because it's obvious if you are not.

BREAKING DOWN THE WALL

When you get in to a relationship you're taking a risk. Throughout the relationship there are numerous risks that you'll face. A classic mistake that is made is people not letting the other person in. Not letting them get close enough to love you. The fear being that if they get close enough to love you, they can get close enough to hurt you. You can't go to Vegas and expect to win the jackpot if you don't place a bet. And if you do place that bet, there is no guarantee that you will win. The smart gambler will tell you not to throw all your chips on the table at once (unless you're playing blackjack on Party Poker, but that's different.) You don't have to let the person in all at once. Like anything else, take your time but realize that your relationship will only grow as much as you allow it to.

I've been in a ton of relationships (more than I'd like to admit), and with every kind of girl. I can tell you with all honesty the most enjoyable time I ever had in any relationship had little to do with sex. Hard to believe, right? It's true, the most magical time for me went like this; I was driving my girlfriend and I home from the bar. It was snowing pretty badly, with some freezing rain mixed in. For some reason, unknown to me, she wanted to make out while we drove, nothing wrong with a little excitement, right? Anyway we get to her grandparents house, which is where she was staying at the time. We sat in the driveway and talked for hours. It was a meaningful talk, we spoke about us. She struggled to tell me she loved me for the first time, even though I jumped the gun a little and said it week or so before. We did nothing more than kiss a little and talk that night. But she opened up to me, she was a really guarded person, her last relationship had gone bad after like two or three years. Her opening up meant more to me than any sexual encounter I've ever had. Except for maybe the first time I watched Midget porn, but it's hard to compete with that.

The point is that some of the greatest moments you'll ever have in your life will have very little to do with anything physical. It could be an all night conversation on the phone or on the computer, or while you hold each other on the couch. Those moments when someone takes a chance to share themselves emotionally with you are the ones to die for. When someone opens up and lets you in to who they really are, those moments are moving in a way that could never be matched physically. I'm still not sold on this whole meeting someone on the internet thing, but I will say that meeting someone online takes away a lot of the physical bullshit and would give you a chance to really get to know them emotionally before the physical stuff comes and messes it all up.

Don't be afraid to open up to someone once they have gained some of your trust. If you shut everyone out, and stop them from getting close to you, how do you expect to find love? How do you expect to be happy if no one knows the real you? I know it means taking a gigantic risk and who am I to tell you what to do with your feelings. I'm a nobody as far as that is concerned (even though I am kind of a big deal), but I'm a person from that same mold. The US military couldn't break down the wall that I have built up around me. Because of that very fact, I have missed out on some really wonderful women along the way. I don't believe in regrets but I do believe in learning from my mistakes. I have shut people out my whole life, which is why I am single.

What is that old saying, "No pain, No gain". I don't know that I'd call it pain, but there is a chance you could end up in emotional pain. You can't get anywhere in life never taking a chance at all. Like my Basketball coach said, you'll miss every shot you don't take. Be selective, but don't be afraid to take a chance on someone. If not you'll end up looking back and wondering 'What if'.

Guys, you shouldn't be afraid to admit your feelings either. No matter if it's happy, sad, afraid or even horny. The number one complaint that women make is that their guy doesn't open up. "He never tells me how he feels." I'm not saying you have to become a poet or memorize the words to Sleepless in Seattle. But find that emotional side to yourself and don't be afraid to open up and share it with her. It can be really simple actually; you'd be surprised how far the little things go. If she's there to support you before a big presentation at work, explain to her that you're nervous and why. It amazes people how talking about basic feelings can ease some of the anxiety and nerves. Or say the Red Sox just won the World Series, (unlikely to happen again much before 2091) explain to her how excited you are and let her share in that excitement. Girls often don't fall in love with their sports teams like guys do (god love the ones that do).

You never want to be afraid to show your emotions, whether it's smiling or crying. Obviously don't make either an overwhelming habit, because no one likes an overly happy person or a crybaby. You showing emotion puts merit to things that you say. Your words now have feelings behind them, makes them a little more meaningful. Don't be afraid to compliment her, but don't just say "Hey your hair looks great." No dig a little deeper with it, and tell her why. "I love it when your hair is curly like that, not sure why but it really turns me on."

Girls, you need to let us scratch a bit deeper then the surface, you tend to build up some really high walls around yourself. I'm sorry your last boyfriend cheated on you with some girl who hardly speaks English. He's an asshole, but at the same time I'm not him. It's his loss anyway right? Tell me what you want from life, where you thought you'd be by now and where you want to be tomorrow, next week, a year from now? Share with me the simple things that make you smile and the major things that piss you off? That's what we want to know, we want to know the things we can't find out from one of your friends. Tell me why you think Justin Timberlake is hot, or why you think Christina Aguilera is a whore (though I will argue that one with you.) These things sound so basic but they tell me about you. That's really not so bad is it? Little by little let me understand the real you. Clearly I will never completely understand you, you are just too complex—and we as guys accept that. You should accept the same thing about us, we are a bit more complex than you think, it's not all sports, sex and beer. But if we do invite you to join us for the sports and beer part, please don't insult us by saying no. It's a very meaningful part of our lives, and this is a way of us trying to open up to you. You may not like the sport or even know anything about it, but I can guarantee you'll never have more fun than you will on a mid-summer Sunday at Fenway Park with some good friends and $10 beers, while the Yankees sweep the Sox to take over first place. You saying no would be the equivalent of us saying no to watching your favorite movie or going shopping.

We are clearly different creatures, from fairly different worlds. But that's the great part of relationships; they pull those two worlds together to make one. When "You and Me" becomes "us". To do that you both will have to open up and let the other person be a part of who you are. It won't be easy, but then the most rewarding things in life are rarely easy.

I myself let people get close to a point. They might scratch at the surface a little, but as soon as it seems like they might break in I cut them off. Just one of the many reasons I'm single, but whatever, I'm over it!

THE LITTLE THINGS

The little things in relationships are what keep it going, whether you've been together dating for a year or married for ten years. People by nature just seem to become complacent; they see no need to put the effort in to something that isn't causing them any pain or stress. Simply, if It's not broken, don't fix it. Why is that, why not strive for better? Sometimes I think we fear change too much; with relationships it's usually not a change that needs to happen. In most cases you need to go back to doing the little things that got you here. Fellas when was the last time you bought her flowers for no reason at all? When was the last time you bought them period? When was the last time you took her out to a nice dinner on a whim? Ladies when was the last time you tried to outdo yourself when making dinner or got dressed up just to impress us? What I'm getting at here is that these are all things that we do early on in a relationship, they are so common they are almost expected. But for some reason after a little time we stop doing it, we stop trying to impress the other person. That should never happen——you should blow each other's minds on a consistent basis. You don't want to do something like this every day that kind of tarnishes the special feeling.

Everyone likes to be treated like a King or a Queen once in a while. You don't even have to be involved in it to blow their mind.

Fella's blind fold her and drive her to the spa, and tell her to enjoy the day—on you, of course. Ladies stock up the fridge with beer and wings, tell him to invite his friends over to watch the game. Just do something special for them.

Think of it this way—compare your relationship to a bodybuilder. Say he or she starts out bench-pressing 150lbs. Over six months he or she works their way up to 300lbs. Should they stop there and just be happy because they've doubled their original weight? No, they set new goals and try to shatter them. Congratulations you made it a year together, now what? The story ends, the book closes, the games over?

It's important to try new things as often as possible, some together and some on your own. It will help keep life ever changing, stop things from becoming mind numbing. If your relationship ever becomes boring, or feels like it just doesn't have any life to it, you need to either spice things up or move on. For some people, a year is all they got, when they hit that wall it's over, there is nothing more. At that point they need to recognize it and cut the strings, no sense in wasting each other's time more than you already have.

Women love the little things. I think they appreciate them a bit more then us guys do. Buy her flowers, give her a massage yourself, or run her a bubble bath. And do these things for no reason, that's what will make them so special. Tell her how great she looks, even if she's just wearing a pair of sweat pants and a hoody. These are all simple things, but are so meaningful to women, it makes them feel appreciated, something we often don't do enough. These are the type of things they want; they don't want to have to ask for it, they want you to just do it. Most things require very little work or effort on your part, but the thought goes further than you could ever imagine. A little something you could do that will benefit you also is to go out and buy her a nice lingerie piece.

Cook the only meal you know how to make, buy a nice bottle of wine and what do you know you've put a little romance back in things. If you want to throw a massage in there you will never regret it.

The little things will keep the relationship alive. Even if you have to mark your personal calendar twice a month to remind you to do something special for them, it's well worth it. But don't do it so that they come to expect things at a certain time or the same day every month, that will take a bit of the surprise and excitement out of it. Being predictable is very boring.

The little things don't need to be physical; you can do so much with words. Tell them they look great or randomly tell them how much you love and care about them, or how happy they make you. Don't just say it damn it-mean it. Love is a powerful thing and you can become content with it and not realize its true power until it's taken away from you. Doing the little things should ensure you never take the other person for granted.

I have taken people for granted before because of my ego and high confidence. I can, at times, get a little too into myself. I starting thinking about how there are so many fish in the sea and keep telling myself that I'm fishing with the best bait there is. But it has cost me some really great girls, because I started to take for granted that they'd always be there. That was certainly not the case at all. Guys, don't treat the ladies that way, and ladies don't put up with it and vice versa—we both deserve much more respect than that.

The little things seem so small and simple, yet so many people ignore the importance of them in a relationship. If things are always a same in the relationship it's going to get boring no matter how much you love the person. Life is too short to spend it being bored.

IT'S NOT YOU, IT'S ME

Not every relationship works out, hell most of them don't. Think about it for a moment, relationships are trial and error. You'll have a bunch of relationships fail before you have the last one. So then comes in to play the "break up". It's really an important part of the whole relationship saga—there always has to be an ending. And while "till death do us part", might be it for some, there will come a time when you need to show the other person the door.

For some people, breaking another person's heart is an effortless act. It may come as a surprise to most women but men often struggle when it comes to actually breaking up with a girl. I have seen guys stick in a relationship two years longer than he should have. He even mentioned breaking up with her, but he just couldn't do it. He tried so many different things to end it without having to actually say it himself. He gave a half assed effort for about 6 months, hoping she'd one day just blame everything on him and end it. But it didn't work, this went on for another 18 months before he finally found his testicles and ended it. Now, both of them stuck around. He wasn't happy and she couldn't have been happy, not with the way he was acting. They stuck with it for different reason.

The guy stayed for a few reasons, first that he doesn't want to be 'that mean guy'. More than most women realize guys care a great deal about how people perceive them. Not just right now, but how he'll be remembered, and no guy wants to be remembered as 'The Asshole'. The second reason can be a little disheartening; guys don't like to move on until they have something else lined up. In a national survey it was found that 25% of guys say they are on the lookout for a better relationship while they are in the one they are in. 25% isn't that high of a number if you're a guy, if you're a girl you are already kicking your guys ass thinking he is part of that 25%. Give him a little more credit than that, please and thank you.

The girl stayed for some of the same reasons, she doesn't want to be 'the bitch'. At the same time, she is a little more ok with that label than the guy is. The majority of the reason the girl stayed is that she loves him, and thinks that she can change him. Tame the wild horse, if you will. That is one of the reasons why some women get with the guy they know is a player, they think they can make him change. It usually leads to them being heartbroken and in the exact same place they were from the start, alone.

Someone grow a pair of balls and stomp all over the other ones heart for god sake. That sounds mean as hell right? But listen, life is nowhere near as long as people seem to think it is. Your shelf life as far as date-ability isn't only from 18-60. But after that, you have to bring Viagra and Depends in to the equation and that can get messy. So stop wasting each other's time and end it for god's sake (if for nothings else, so the rest of us can have some good rebound sex.)

-When You Should Dump HIM-

Ladies do you ever wonder if maybe you over reacted when you dumped him? If it was me you dumped, you certainly did over react you cold, heartless, she devil! Now, obviously if he cheated or got physical with you, kick his ass to the curb and do it now. Here are some other reasons to part ways and get on with your life. Remember you have a lot to offer, and he's not the only one out there.

If he's ignoring you, don't be afraid to show him the door. But make sure he's ignoring you and that he's just not listening. The difference? A guy that ignores you consistently forgets the important things, Birthday's, Anniversary's, or he puts himself in front of the 'us' moments. For example, he doesn't do anything for you on your birthday because The Sox and Yankees are on ESPN. That's just Selfish and you don't have to put up with it. This refers to big issues, not him forgetting to put the toilet seat down or not getting the right tampons at the store. If he's ignoring you, boot him. If he has ADHD and is a little slow, work with him a bit.

If he's leading two lives you need to give him his walking papers and send him on his way. If you've never meet his friends or been to his place, something's wrong and you need to fix it with your foot to his ass. If he says he is working late, consider the situation. If he's working at Foot Locker and the store closes at 9 and he's not strolling in till midnight saying he was working, something's up. But if he works for some Marketing Firm and he's got a big project coming up chances are pretty good he's actually working.

If he becomes the crazy stalker boyfriend? We all need our space; you need yours as much as he needs his. If he won't let you out of the house to check the mail without clearing it with him first, stick a fork in him, he's done! There is a thin line between a guy being protective and a guying being psycho stalker. If he asks what you're doing today, or who you were with at the mall shopping, it is more than likely he's just trying to start a conversation or trying to keep involved in your life. But if he calls more then 10 times a day just "to see where you are?" You need to cut him loose right away. Guys like this can be suffocating and often times, it leads to physically and emotionally abusive relationships

This last reason is very situational. Another reason you should dump him in a second is if I happen to ask you out. If you are lucky enough for this to happen to you, under no circumstances do you say no to me, you run home and tell him it's over…Even if it's just for a night.

Breaking up with someone is never an easy thing to do. It gets emotional and can be very straining on you personally but it is vital to your happiness. So, it may suck today, but you have to think about tomorrow. By that I mean look at things in the long run. If he's not treating you right he doesn't deserve you anyway.

-When You Should Dump HER-

Women can be complicated but don't over think things. If she messes up badly she's got to go. Don't let her lure you back with her emotional guilt trip or her great breasts. If she's getting something on the side she's got to go——no questions asked. Here are some other things that she deserves the boot for and don't be too much of a pussy to do it either.

If she's more interested in finding a husband than finding out about you, it's time to bail out my good man. It's one thing to bring up how she wants to get married *someday* but it's another if every conversation leads back to her wanting to be married and her clock ticking, you need to move on. This is to much pressure, especially if this is a new relationship. Big deal if her clock is ticking, so is everyone else's, and unless she's about to pass away her clock will keep ticking. If she isn't interested in who you are and what you're about, then, my friend, you are merely a penis and a wedding ring. I assure you the ring will get much more action then you will in the long run.

She's choking the shit out of you. By this I mean you haven't taken a piss without her over your shoulder asking you what you're doing. Some women (and men) can become very suffocating and controlling. These are usually the really jealous type, they want to know where you are every second of the day. They count the number of condoms in the box and keep a written inventory of each time you had sex, pray to god that box doesn't come up short. You have a life to live, and you can't do that with someone stuck to you 24/7. Cut the strings and get on with things.

If she's looking for an ass kisser. Listen, if a girl wants you to do nothing but kiss her ass all the time, you need to step off and kick her ass out the door. How demoralizing is that shit, she might be great and all, but she does not need to hear it all the time. She needs to respect you, more importantly you need to respect you. Don't let her treat you like some servant.

This is probably the best reason to break up with her, and it's really not even her fault. Look, if she meets me and I hit on her, you're just never going to measure up again, sorry. But listen, chances are I'll mess it up in a week or two so be there for the rebound and you're in like Flynn.

Guys have gotten the reputation as the ones who always mess everything up, girls mess up just as much as we guys do. They just don't get held accountable like guys do. If she isn't going to respect you and see you for the great guy that you are then you're too good for her.

-How to Break Their Heart!-

Forget about trying that whole 'lets just be friend's' garbage. Here is why it never works, guys have a really hard time being just friends, and especially if we've had sex. We will still want to have sex, just as friends, of course. Girls have a hard time seeing guys with other girls. So throw that whole "let's just be friends" speech out the window right now. There would be a lot more honestly in you saying "You just don't do it for me, we'll probably never have another comfortable conversation again. But hey, it's been fun, head up kid, you'll meet someone else."

Now that we've taken out the trash, let's get to some important points. First, don't you dare do it any other way than face to face. Not in a letter, not on the phone, no email or text messages and definitely don't have someone else do it. No matter how long the relationship has lasted you owe that person the respect of breaking their heart while you look them in the eye. Face to face, eye to eye in a private place. Don't do it at a bar or restaurant or with a bunch of friends in the car to help avoid the other person making a scene.

A question you should ask yourself before you make the move to break their heart. *Why?* What is the real reason and make sure it's for you and not because your friends don't like the person. Don't get me wrong, what your friends think is important, but if you really care about a person you need to do what is best for you.

Don't lie about the "why". If you met someone else then say so, you cheating son of a bitch. If it is because they cheated they should already know. No matter the reason, even if it's because the sex is so bad you can't even get yourself off in the bathroom after you faked it. Obviously, it's always good to say it in the nicest possible way. You don't want to be cruel when you're letting them down easy. You want to maintain a bit of politeness for a few reasons. The first being that you could realize a week or so later that you made a monumental mistake and you now want them back. If you did nothing but insult them the whole time you gave them the boot, your chances of reconciliation are slim. The second reason is that people talk. You don't want to be considered an asshole, especially if you live in a small town or she has a lot of hot friends. The third reason, and maybe the most meaningful one, is respect. You've spent some quality time with them, maybe have some really good memories; you don't want to taint them with hatred.

The third and most important thing to remember is not to let them suck you back in. It wasn't working for you for a reason, and once you explain it to them they will more than likely plea for you to give them another chance, promise that they'll change. They may even cry, that's when I get weak. They start crying and I start to feel bad. But you can't, you need to hold your ground. If they promise to change, tell them they need to change first, then come and talk to you about having another go at it. Every time I think about this, I think about the girl who has finally mustered up the courage to kick the cheating or beating boyfriend to the curb. He begs, and swears he'll change, he cries, tells her how much he needs her. And how long does all of that last? Not long and he's back to cheating or beating all over again. Get out as soon as you can ladies, you can never love someone enough to take that kind of physical or mental abuse. You're all princess's and deserve to be treated that way.

There is an old philosophy that you break up with them before they break up with you. I have mixed emotions about this theory.

There really isn't such a thing as a mutual split, someone had to initiate it. So who breaks who's heart? If you ask me, and you obviously are because you're reading my book, if you are not happy, then you need to do it. Don't do it just to beat them to the punch. The argument is that if you are the one who breaks it off you have control, and have now placed the emotional strain on the other person. I'm not sold on that idea myself. I've broken up with girls and think that I've felt worse afterward than they did. One of them went out on a date the very next night, while I was at home watching Animal Planet and thinking about all the kinky places we'd had sex. But other times I've been the one who was broken up with and sat at home feeling like hell for weeks at a time.

On a serious note some people believe the break up can be a very useful tool to a relationship. It's very risky but can be very beneficial. Say things have hit a wall, things have gotten boring—you love each other but maybe wonder how far that love will carry you. Take a break! You're taking a big risk by suggesting it, but it could also make you both realize what the other one means to you. It's a huge gamble but after a week if you're going crazy because you miss them, then you know that what you have is something at least semi-real, from your perspective that is. The risk is what effect the break up will have on them. Relationships in themselves are a risk, but you're taking a serious risk here, because there is a real chance that they won't come back to you.

The last bit of advice I want to leave you with about breaking up is do not, I repeat DO NOT UNDER ANY CIRCUM-STANCES use the line "It's not you, it's me." That is my line.

-Surviving the Break Up-

A few other things about breaking up; let's say you're the one who's just gotten dumped—they weren't all that great anyway.

How long should you take to grieve or sit around being depressed about it? No more than a week. I know, I know that is hardly any time at all to get over someone you just spent a significant amount of time with. No one is telling you to just get over it, what I am saying is that you need to make an attempt to move on with your life. Life is rather fast paced and you need to keep up with it. Sitting at home watching midget porn or eating Ben n Jerry's is not the answer. First thing you do, and this is going to sound really corny, but after you do it you'll realize the effect it has on you. Get in front of the mirror (I like to do it naked, but that's just me), take a minute and just stare at yourself, look yourself in the eye for a good minute or so, Then say "Fuck it, their loss!" Don't mumble it; say it like you mean it. Remember how important I said confidence is when it comes to meeting someone, well it's just as important when it comes to getting over someone.

The next thing you need after the mirror session is your friends. You need them to help you get on with things. Guys and girls do this a little different, guys will go out, get drunk, maybe hit the strip club. While girls will have a ladies night at home where they order Chinese food, drink a few bottles of wine and eat ice cream from the container. You need your friends even if you aren't in the mood to be around people or to do anything. Your friends are your crutch, don't be afraid to lean on them a little, they'll help you through without ever having to talk about that person you're trying to forget. Go to the club or go catch a ball game or a movie. Don't just sit at home; it'll only make things worse. You'd be surprised how fast you can move on when you meet someone else. Then Mr. /Ms. Right-now turns in to Mr./Ms. Right, and before you know it you're forgetting about how miserable you were when so and so broke your heart. Now I'm not saying go out and hop in bed with someone the first chance you get. Although rebound sex can be very helpful, it may help you realize what else is really out there.

Now for a sad and pathetic story; I once dated this girl for only a few months. Then suddenly after my 4th of July party, I don't hear from her again for two weeks. I called, I emailed, even sent her flowers to her work. Then one day I get an email saying, "I need my space." An email, I don't get a chance to ask any questions, no eye contact, hell I didn't even get the chance to reel her back in. I'm sitting there wondering what the hell the last two weeks has been, seemed like space to me. In reality it rocked me, and rocked me hard. I was seriously in to this girl and I never got a real answer. This is how my life went for that whole summer; Sunday thru Wednesday I sat at home, worked very little, watched a lot of television, and spent hours on end sitting at the computer hoping she would log on to AOL messenger so I could ask her why. Thursday, Friday and Saturday I was in Canada with the Fellas hitting every bar and club we could find acting like there was nothing at all wrong with me. Towards the end of the summer as I'm finally starting to come out of my daze, some friends and I going tubing down the river and who do we see on the walking path but this she devil herself with who else but her ex-boyfriend. Just needed some space my ass! That whole ex-boyfriend thing seems to happen to me a lot. Anyway after a few more weeks of drinking and drunk Canadian girls who spoke little English I was as good as new.

Someone really stupid once said, "It's better to love and have lost than to have never loved at all." So it's better to go to Vegas and lose all your money than to have never gone to Vegas at all? It just doesn't make much sense, neither of the situations. I would have never felt the great feeling of love if I would have known someone was going to come and take it away. Love is such a powerful emotion that to have it taken away is a life altering event, assuming that what you're feeling is really love. But then again, the great memories from a loving relationship are irreplaceable. So make up your own mind on that one. Hopefully it's never an issue. Hopefully your one of the lucky ones that never has to lose.

AND I'M SPENT

We all have a common goal, a common understanding of one thing we want to get in life, and that is love. There is no secret treasure map that is going to lead you to that promise land. We are all different people with different goals and objectives in life. Finding the right person that will fit in to our goals is not an easy task, and I don't want you to believe that by reading this book that it is just suddenly going to happen. What I will promise you is that this book will provide you with some valuable information that will help you along the way. I'm in hopes that some of the situations that I have been in can serve to be helpful for you. I'd like to hope I didn't go through all that for nothing and that someone can learn from it.

I have been in some great relationships and I have been in ones that should have never made it past the introductions. But that's what life is about, trial and error, it's rare that you'll get it right on the first try so don't be afraid to fail. Yes there is many risks you take when you open yourself up to people, but when are you not taking a risk in life? Think of all the risks you take in life, eating the peanuts that have been sitting in a bowl on the bar for god knows how long, sitting on a public toilet seat or not looking both ways before you cross the road. Those risks have little to no reward to you, you're taking a gamble and getting nothing out of it. With love you can reap serious rewards, emotionally, physically and every other aspect of your life. So you have to put yourself out there a little, but it's worth it.

Putting yourself out there becomes a lot easier when you believe in yourself and what you can bring to the table. The reality is if you don't believe in you, there is no way anyone else can. You kind of have to love yourself before you can love anyone else, it sounds cheesy but it's true. If you can't even love you how in the world can you love someone else; I just don't see it to be possible. People talk about the secret to success, this is it—confidence. If you believe in yourself, the sky is really the limit. Don't be afraid to be yourself and feel confident about whom that person is. You really do have something to offer to anyone out there, you just have to believe in it and yourself enough to start selling it to people.

I hope that, if nothing else, you laughed a lot reading this book. I assure you that all the stories are authentic; really I couldn't make stuff like this up if I tried. This book has actually been kind of therapeutic for me. You'll have noticed that I remarked a lot about me being single, in the beginning it was a humor thing, something to make people laugh, but as I went on writing I started to realize all the things I have done over the years to so many of my relationships. I think I might have sabotaged myself a little. Maybe it just wasn't the right time for me or maybe love just scared the shit out of me. I sit back and wonder sometimes if maybe I missed the right one for me, maybe I missed the real love of my life. Could life be that cruel, it certainly can as Ervin showed you when he had to have stitches in his penis (it really doesn't get much crueler than that does it?)

In closing I wish you luck in finding that person, who is perfect for you, whether you find them in a bar while you're watching the Yankee's beat the Red Sox or at a club with Sisqo's *Thong Song* blasting in the background. The important part is that you find them. And if you can't seem to locate them, and you have a sexual need that you must please, pick up my next book which will be a guide to the one night stand. Hey, I'm single for a reason.

CPSIA information can be obtained at www.ICGtesting.com
Printed in the USA
LVOW040715250912

300199LV00001B/163/P